D1072742

Machines at Work

Concrete Mixers

by Cari Meister

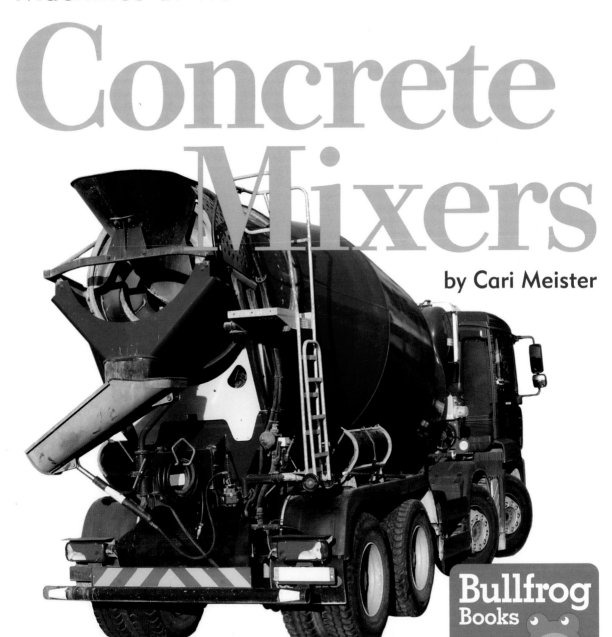

Bullfrog Books

Ideas for Parents and Teachers

Bullfrog Books let children practice reading informational text at the earliest reading levels. Repetition, familiar words, and photo labels support early readers.

Before Reading

• Discuss the cover photo. What does it tell them?

• Look at the picture glossary together. Read and discuss the words.

Read the Book

• "Walk" through the book and look at the photos. Let the child ask questions. Point out the photo labels.

• Read the book to the child, or have him or her read independently.

After Reading

• Prompt the child to think more. Ask: Have you ever seen a concrete mixer? Do you know what the concrete was being used for?

Bullfrog Books are published by Jump!
5357 Penn Avenue South
Minneapolis, MN 55419
www.jumplibrary.com

Library of Congress Cataloging-in-Publication Data

Names: Meister, Cari.
Title: Concrete mixers / by Cari Meister.
Description: Minneapolis, MN: Jump!, Inc., [2017]
Series: Machines at work
Audience: Ages 5–8. | Audience: K to Grade 3.
Includes index.
Identifiers: LCCN 2016002944 (print)
LCCN 2016012036 (ebook)
ISBN 9781620313664 (hardcover: alk. paper)
ISBN 9781620314845 (paperback)
ISBN 9781624964138 (ebook)
Subjects: LCSH: Concrete mixers—Juvenile literature.
Classification: LCC TA439 .M366 2017 (print)
LCC TA439 (ebook) | DDC 629.225—dc23
LC record available at http://lccn.loc.gov/2016002944

Editor: Jenny Fretland VanVoorst
Series Designer: Ellen Huber
Book Designer: Leah Sanders
Photo Researcher: Leah Sanders

Photo Credits: All photos by Shutterstock except: Adobe Stock, 22, 24; Aisyaqilumar2/Shutterstock.com, 9; Getty Images, 18, 23bl; Glow Images, cover; Omega Concrete Mixers, 12–13; Sergei Butorin/Shutterstock.com, 5.

Printed in the United States of America at Corporate Graphics in North Mankato, Minnesota.

Table of Contents

A Mixer at Work

Bo drives a concrete mixer.

He is at the plant.

He needs concrete for a job.

5

Beep! Beep!
He backs up.

The hopper opens.

hopper

Cement goes in.
Water goes in.
Rocks go in.

9

It has a drum.

The drum spins.

That way the concrete inside does not dry.

drum

lever

AUXILIARY

WATER

9
8
7
6
5
4
3
2
1
0

EMERGENCY
STOP

CO

CEMENT
SPEED

VIBRATORS
1 2

3   4

Bo pulls a lever.

The things inside mix.

Vroom!

He drives
to the job site.

They are
making a floor.

At the job site,
Bo puts on a chute.

chute

He pulls a lever.

Look!

Concrete comes out.

It is wet.

Soon it will dry.

The job is done.
Nice work!

Parts of a Concrete Mixer

hopper
The place materials are put in the mixer.

drum
The spinning container that holds concrete.

chute
The slide where concrete comes out.

cab
The place where the driver sits.

Picture Glossary

cement
A soft powder that is mixed with other things to make concrete.

lever
A bar that is used to open and close something.

concrete
A strong material made from mixing rocks, water, and cement together.

plant
A factory where something is made.

Index

To Learn More

Learning more is as easy as 1, 2, 3.

1) Go to www.factsurfer.com

2) Enter "concretemixers" into the search box.

3) Click the "Surf" button to see a list of websites.

With factsurfer.com, finding more information is just a click away.